MONEY
MEDITATION
MANIFESTATION!

The 7 Strategies That Manifest Money Fast!

By: Christopher Mitchell

www.ChangeYourLifeOvernight.com

MONEY MEDITATION MANIFESTATION!
The 7 Strategies That Manifest Money Fast!

Copyright © 2017 Christopher Mitchell

ISBN-13: 978-1546584841

ISBN-10: 1546584846

Printed In The United States Of America.

TABLE OF CONTENTS:

Let me teach you how to become a Self-Published Author in record time! It's fast, cheap, and simple! I'll send you all my best Stats, Facts, & Tips **ABSOLUTELY FREE**! The only thing you need to do is submit your name and email address right here:

www.ChangeYourLifeOvernight.com

Chapter One:

Facts About Money!

Fact: Money is the answer for EVERYTHING! It even says so in the Holy Bible in this verse right here:

A feast is made for laughter, wine makes life merry, and money is the answer for everything.
Ecclesiastes 10:19

It's something everyone already knows, but no one wants to admit it because we've been taught that money is bad and it's noble to be poor. Well, I'm here to talk about money a lot and to say that being poor is a sin and a disgrace to humanity, especially if you're an American, where The United States Of America is the land of opportunity. My goal for writing this book is to change your mind set about money.

Fact: If you earn just $32,400 a year then you're in the top 1% of money earners in the entire world.

I know that sounds crazy, but odds are you're probably an American who lives in The United States. If so, you don't understand how poor the rest of the world outside our country really is. Though our country has more millionaires and billionaires than any other country on the planet, there are still more than two million Americans who live on less than two dollars a day. Throughout the world there are more than three billion people who live on less than two dollars a day. So, like I said, if you're an American citizen you're more than likely in the top 1% of money earners in the entire world. Consider yourself blessed beyond measure. Once you realize how blessed you already are more money will start to flow to you.

Though earning just $32,400 a year will put you in the top 1% of money earners in the world globally, that same amount will have you living at the poverty level in America. To make your way into the top 1% of money earners in America will require you to earn $429,000 a year.

Fact: A whopping 98% of the population in America will either be dead or dead broke by the time they reach sixty-five years old.

You must remember that the numbers I've listed in this book are facts, not my opinion. More people move to America than any other country in the world because this is the land of opportunity. They know that if they can just step foot on American soil they can become rich beyond their wildest imagination. However, 98% of the people born and raised in America are dead broke. This is their choice by the way. Being rich or poor is simply a choice. It's a choice to work at a job for someone else as an employee rather than being an entrepreneur and owning a business. So, if you choose to be an employee rather than choose to be a business owner, you're making the choice to be poor. Look at the facts:

Fact: 98% of America's population is dead broke!

Fact: 98% of America's population are employees!

Fact: 2% of America's population is wealthy!

Fact: 2% of America's population are business owners!

Fact: If you want to get rich and have a lot of money you must become an entrepreneur and own a business.

If so many people in the world dream of coming to America so they can get filthy, stinkin rich, then why are 98% of the people born and raised in America dead broke? I believe this problem exists because of all the following reasons:

-Americans are just downright lazy. They have no work ethic.

-We learn from our parents and our environments. Poverty breeds more poverty. This is a generational curse.

-Americans have an entitlement mentality where they expect the government to take care of them.

-The public-school system doesn't teach students anything about hard work, entrepreneurship, starting your own business, or how to invest your money and make it grow.

-Americans waste more of their time watching the stupid box than any other place in the world. Television mentally programs people to live in fear and abject poverty.

The culture that people grow up in outside of America is quite different. When I lived in Los Angeles for fifteen years I met many people from other countries. Every single one of them were business owners. Let me tell you about one family that stands out in my mind the most.

I knew a Hispanic couple who came to America with their four children from Mexico. They had saved every single penny they had (or peso) for several years. Once they arrived in America they used all of their money to open up their own Mexican restaurant. They didn't have any money left for housing, so all six of them lived inside their restaurant. They slept on the floor of the kitchen. As a family, they all worked together. They would wake up at 8:00 in the morning to prepare the restaurant for the day. They wouldn't go to bed at night until the restaurant was cleaned, which was about 2:00 in the morning. All six of them lived this way every single day for the first three years that they lived in America.

However, their sacrifice paid off. They are now multi-millionaires. They now own several businesses, they own several real estate properties, they don't have any debt, and they are truly living the American dream. Most of the people born and raised in America would never do that. The majority of the population in America make too many excuses, while people from other countries just take action and make things happen.

This proves that if you want to get rich and have a lot of money, nothing can stop you if you'll just get to work and be willing to make sacrifices. You've got to stop making excuses though. You can make money or you can make excuses, but you can't make both. So, choose one!

Fact: The wealthiest 85 people on the planet have more money than the poorest 3.5 billion people combined.

Now, instead of condemning the rich because they have so much money, how about you become rich so you can help the poor get out of poverty. Having a lot of money is nothing more than having a positive mindset about it. Yes, America absolutely has more opportunities available to you than any other place in the world, however, anyone can change their life financially if they'll just use their creativity and not feel sorry for themselves. That's also why I decided to write this book. If the poor people in the world can get their hands on this book then they can start thinking differently about money. Once they start thinking differently money will start to come to them in ways that are currently unimaginable to them.

There is no shortage of money in the world. That's the first thing I want you to start focusing on. Once you realize we live in a world of absolute abundance, then all you need to do is start creating ways to have that abundance come to you. Think of different businesses you can start. If you want to have a lot of money you must own a business.

Fact: 90% of employees in America only earn $28,000 a year in income.

If you want to have a lot of money you must start changing the way you think about money. If you want to have a lot of money you absolutely must become an entrepreneur. If you want to have millions of dollars in your bank account, if you want to drive your dream cars, if you want to live in a 10,000 square foot mansion, if you want to take vacations all over the world, and if you want to be free of all debt, you absolutely must become an entrepreneur.

Employees will never become rich. You must accept this fact and start your own business. If you don't ever plan on starting your own business, then you need to be content with being poor for the rest of your life.

Fact: You will never get rich and have a lot of money by being an employee.

If you want to have a lot of money you absolutely must eliminate any debt that you have. Debt will keep you living in slavery and bondage forever. Car payments, mortgage payments, credit card payments, and anything else that charges you monthly interest will never allow you to get rich. Pay these things off for good, and once you do, don't ever borrow money again. If you can't afford to pay cash for something then don't get it. Don't live a life of slavery just so you can try to impress others.

Fact: The average household in America has $16,748 of credit card debt.

Fact: The average household in America has $28,948 of car loan debt.

Fact: The average household in America has $49,905 of student loan debt.

Fact: The average household in America has $176,222 of mortgage loan debt.

If you add all that debt up, it comes to a grand total of $271,823. Then, if you consider that the average household in America only brings in about $52,000 per year, you can see how it is practically impossible for the average family to ever get out of debt. If they can't get themselves out of debt then they will never get rich and have a lot of money.

Keep reading! In the following chapters I'm going to share some proven strategies with you that will teach you how to bring in a lot more money so that you can get out of debt as soon as possible and start living the American dream.

Chapter Two:

Importance Of Money!

I know that you already know that money is important, but have you ever taken into consideration just how important it is? Probably not, because most people take it for granted. Like the Holy Bible says, money is the answer for everything! I completely agree with this and you should too. It's the truth!

Money is just like oxygen, you can't live without it. In third world countries people die because of starvation. The reason why they starved is because they didn't have any money. People will break into a bank hoping that they can get some money. People will kill other human beings so they can take their money by robbing them or hoping to cash in on a life insurance policy. People claim other people's kids on their tax returns so that they can get more money back. People work two and three jobs because they want or need more money. People will take every penny they have and gamble it away hoping to win a bigger amount of money. People known as gold diggers will pretend to love another human being only to use them for their money. People will make up lies and create illegal ponzi schemes to cheat people out of their money for their own gain. People will even become prostitutes and have sex for money.

Now, do you see how important money really is? People will do anything for money. That's why it's important to get rich, because if you don't have a lot of money it will become your God. It will rule you. A lack of money will consume your life.

My favorite book in the world is the Holy Bible. It's filled with wisdom and it talks a lot about money. I'm going to share many scriptures with you throughout this book about money. If you'll read and study the Holy Bible it will teach you how to get rich so you can have a lot of money. I've noticed throughout my life that the number one thing on the minds of broke people is money. They stress out about it and worry about not having any. When people are stressed out about money and they're constantly worried about it, they make money into an idol and it becomes their God. You never want to make money your God. Money is a wonderful servant, but a terrible master. You need to control money rather than allow it to control you. Let me show you what it says in the Holy Bible about money being your master:

No one can serve two masters. Either you will hate the one and love the other, or you will be devoted to the one and despise the other. You cannot serve both God and money.
Matthew 6:24

Money can never bring you God, but God can most certainly bring you money. Please remember that! There's another scripture in the same chapter that proves this to be true:

But seek first his kingdom and his righteousness, and all these things will be given to you as well.
Matthew 6:33

This bible verse is talking about putting God first place in your life. If you do, you can be sure that God will give you all the money and desires of your heart. Money is extremely important for not only survival in this world, but to enjoy everything that life has to offer as well. You just want to make sure that money doesn't become your God. A lot of people will just assume that money is my God because I talk about it so much, but the truth of the matter is that I want to teach people how to get rich and have a lot of money so that:

-They aren't controlled by a lack of money in their lives.

-They don't lose sleep being stressed out about not having any money.

-They don't have to worry about not being able to pay their bills or make ends meet for their families.

-They don't have to break the law or sacrifice their morals and ethics trying to get money.

-They don't constantly fight with their spouse and become another statistic by getting a divorce.

-They can be a blessing to others who are less fortunate who might not have the ability to create money like we have in America.

I've always said that they best thing you can do for the poor is not to be one of them. I have a generous heart and I love giving away money to help the less fortunate, but when I was poor I wasn't able to do that. My number one goal for becoming rich was always to have an abundance of money so that I could give it away to those who were badly in need of it. I hope this is your goal for wanting a lot of money as well.

We must admit to ourselves that money is important. Money dictates everything we do in the world. When a person doesn't have a lot of money life is stressful and difficult. Money creates freedom. I've lived in both poverty and abundance in life, and I can honestly tell you that having an abundance of money makes life less stressful and a hundred times more enjoyable. Everyone knows we can't live without money. However, most people have never experienced what it's like to have a lot of money, so therefore, they don't even believe it's possible to have a lot of money. In order for you to start creating a lot of money after you've been programed to be poor your entire life is going to require you to change your belief system about money. You have to believe that having a lot of money is possible before you'll ever be able to start enjoying it. Let's go to the next chapter. It will increase your faith for bringing in more money.

Chapter Three:

Choose Money!

Numbers don't lie! So, when statistics say that 98% of Americans are poor (live paycheck to paycheck), that's the truth. Since 98% is practically everyone in the country, odds are you know what it's like to be poor yourself. I definitely know what it's like to be poor. I grew up with a mom who died from stress (cancer) because she never had any money. My dad walked out on my mom before she died and he has never had a penny to his name. I'm the first person in my generational blood line to become rich. That was my choice, just like everything else in life is. So, if you want to become rich and have an abundant supply of money, you have to make the same choice that I did. Choose to have a lot of money.

Are you wondering, Christopher, how do I choose to have a lot of money? Well, pay attention and I'll tell you. You choose to have a lot of money by what you do with it. You see, people become rich from what they do with their money. On the other hand, people also become poor from what they do with their money. What you do with your money is your choice. If you're currently broke, busted, disgusted, and can't be trusted with money, it's only because of what you've done with your money up to this point in your life.

If you want to become rich and have an abundant supply of money, all you have to do is start making different choices with your money. What do I mean by making different choices with your money? I mean, do you spend your money or invest your money? If you're poor then I already know what you do with your money. You spend it all just like the other 98% of poor people in the world do. Poor people spend all their money on the most expensive, newest I-phone that comes out. Poor people spend all their money on the most expensive, biggest screen television they can find. Poor people spend all their money on the most expensive car that a bank will finance them for. Poor people spend all their money living in a luxury apartment. That's why they're poor. They choose to be poor by what they spend all their money on.

Rich people on the other hand don't spend their money, they invest it. When you spend your money on an I-phone, big screen television, or drinking beer at happy hour, that money is gone forever. You're never getting it back. However, rich people invest their money in real estate, up and coming entrepreneurs, and the stock market. They don't lose their money like poor people do, they actually multiply it. That's why the rich get richer and the poor get poorer. It's all a matter of choice.

You choose to have a lot of money by what you do with the money you have. Why would you spend $600 on a brand new I-phone when your old cell phone worked just fine? Why would you spend your money on a big screen television when you shouldn't be watching that stupid box at all? Why would you spend your money on a luxury apartment when you could invest it in a house? Why would you spend your money on drinking beer at happy hour when you say you're trying to lose weight? This is why you're poor! You must take responsibility for your spending.

If I told you I started my global book publishing company for only $20, would you believe me? It's true! It was the last $20 I had too. I had a choice to either eat or use the $20 to start a business. Like all rich people, I chose to invest my money in a brand new business. It was the greatest $20 investment that I ever made.

If you want to have a lot of money you have to make that choice. You make that choice by your actions, not your words. Talk is cheap! Actions speak louder than words. It doesn't matter what you say, it matters what you do. What you do with your money from this point forward will determine whether you stay poor or become rich. It's your choice!

Chapter Four:

Tithing Money!

Tithing is not a new concept. To understand tithing you need to know what tithing is. The word "tithe" means tenth. Tithing money is when you give one tenth or 10% of your gross income to your home church. The tithe goes to pay for the church expenses and to further advance The Kingdom Of God. Every rich man I've ever known is a tither. It's a law of success. When you tithe, it gives God, the creator of the entire universe, the legal permission to protect your money from being stolen. Think of tithing as an insurance policy. The greatest insurance policy there is.

You release money everywhere you go, except when you go to church, if you even go to church. When you go to the grocery store you can't walk out without first leaving some money behind. When you go out to eat at a restaurant you can't walk out without first leaving some money behind. When you go to the movie theaters you can't walk out without first leaving some money behind. When you go to a sporting event you can't walk out without first leaving some money behind. Shoot, most of these places won't even allow you to walk in without first giving them some of your money.

However, people will go to church, listen to the Pastor preach an Academy Award winning sermon, and then walk out without giving any of their money whatsoever. That is stinginess! Do you know what the Holy Bible says about stinginess?

The stingy are eager to get rich and are unaware that poverty awaits them. **Proverbs 28:22**

It has been statistically proven that people who tithe have a much higher net worth than people who don't. Tithers have less credit card debt than non-tithers do. Tithers have more cars and homes that are completely paid for than non-tithers do. And, tithers have less health problems than non-tithers do.

What's interesting about this is that a tither looks at tithing and says to himself, I'm better off because I tithe. On the other hand, a non-tither looks at tithing and says to himself, they tithe because they're better off. Tithing is nothing more than a choice, just like everything else. Rich people look at tithing as an investment, poor people look at tithing as an expense.

It's no wonder why they're poor. If you're not a tither you're making another bad choice with your money.

The difference between a tither and a non-tither is in their mindset. The tither looks at the glass and says it's half full. The non-tither looks at the glass and says it's half empty. I would rather my bank account be half full than to have it be half empty. I don't know about you, but I'm going to continue to be a tither. I started tithing when I was a young boy and I'm never going to stop.

When a person gives God 10% of their gross income their money changes kingdoms. It leaves the kingdom of man and enters The Kingdom Of God. When you give God your tithes you're letting him know you trust him. When you give God your tithes you're giving him legal permission to protect your money, but when you don't give God your tithes you're actually robbing him of being able to protect your money.

Return to me and I will return to you says The Lord Almighty. But you ask, how are we to return? Will a mere mortal rob God? Yet, you rob me. But you ask, how are we robbing you? In tithes and offerings. You are under a curse, your whole nation because you are robbing me. Bring the whole tithe into the storehouse, that there may be food in my house. Test me in this says The Lord Almighty and see if I will not throw open the floodgates of Heaven and pour out so much blessing that there will not be room enough to store it. **Malachi 3:7-10**

Tithing isn't a financial issue. It's a trust issue. A tither says, God I trust you to do what you said you would do, so here's a token of my faith. God asks us for our money because he doesn't want money to be our God. Money is a wonderful servant, but a terrible master. Remember that!

No one can serve two masters. Either you will hate the one and love the other, or you will be devoted to the one and despise the other. You cannot serve both God and money.
Matthew 6:24

People say they love and trust God, but he wants to see if your actions back up your words. God knows that actions speak louder than words. Don't say you trust God with your words, but then rob God with your money. You can't lie to God. You'll know when you trust in God because you'll be happy to give him your money in the form of tithes.

If you want to become rich and have a lot of money, I highly encourage you to become a tither. Tithing is like putting a life insurance policy on your money and your material assets. Tithing will protect you from the enemies in the world who try to steal what you have. The greatest thing you could ever do for yourself, your family, and your material assets, is to start tithing. It's better to have 90% of your money blessed, than to have all 100% of your money cursed.

Chapter Five:

Attracting Money!

This chapter is going to teach you how to start attracting money to you through The Law Of Attraction. This powerful, universal law states that whatever you focus on you're going to attract into your life because your thoughts are things.

The Law Of Attraction could also be called the power of focus. What are you constantly focusing on a regular basis? Do you focus on getting bills in the mail every single day, or do you focus on getting paychecks in the mail every single day? You know what the answer is based on what you're getting in the mail every single day.

Have you ever focused on getting caught in a traffic jam? If so, what happened? You got caught in a traffic jam didn't you? Have you ever focused on arriving late to work in the morning? If so, what happened? You arrived late to work didn't you? Have you ever focused on running into an old friend you haven't seen in a long time? If so, what happened? You ran into them didn't you? This is the powerful Law Of Attraction at work in your life. I can always look back to the past and figure out what I was focusing on during that period of time based on what I was attracting into my life.

I remember seeing a beautiful girl with blonde hair sitting in the bleachers when I was sixteen years old playing in one of my baseball games. I stared at her when I walked up to the plate when it was my turn to bat. I stared at her when I was in the field playing shortstop. I stared at her when I ran off the field to the dugout when the innings were over. I had never seen her before, but I couldn't get her out of my mind. I didn't know her name. I didn't know who she was. I didn't even know who she was cheering for. All I knew is that I wanted to meet her, talk to her, and go out on a date with her. By the time the game was over and I packed up my equipment she was gone. She was nowhere to be seen. I thought about her later that night. I thought about her while I was in school. I thought about her when I was at baseball practice. I thought about her all the time.

About a month later, I received a phone call from a girl I didn't know. I asked her who she was since I didn't recognize her voice. She said, I'm the blonde girl that was sitting in the bleachers watching your baseball game about a month ago. What? I yelled in excitement! Are you kidding me? How in the world did you get my phone number? How did you find out who I was? What are you calling me for? She said, I thought you were cute. I wanted to talk to you after your game, but I had to leave. So, I started asking around. Sure enough, I tracked you down. That's amazing I said! I'm so glad you did. I haven't stopped thinking about you since that day. We started dating at that very moment. That was the powerful Law Of Attraction at work in my life. My focused thinking attracted her to me.

That story clearly shows you how powerful our thoughts are. I focused on her for an entire month. She didn't even go to my school, but my laser beam, focused thoughts attracted her into my life. What I focused on, which is known as The Law Of Attraction, worked for me.

As a little boy growing up I loved the Rocky movies played by Sylvester Stallone. I must have watched those movies at least a hundred times. I knew every single word in every movie. I visualized myself being Rocky in the movies. I would punch the same way that he punched. I would talk the same way that he talked. I would even mimic every move that he made. I focused on playing the role of Rocky by Sylvester Stallone so much that he started to dominate my thoughts. I wanted to meet him so badly. I wanted to tell him how much I loved watching his movies.

Well, years later when I was in my twenties I worked as a vendor at a supplement booth in Columbus, Ohio at the annual Arnold Schwarzenegger Bodybuilding Expo. While walking through thousands of people to get to my booth I suddenly came across a huge mob of people blocking all the walk ways. I was surrounded by people and there was nowhere to go. I asked some people crammed up next to me what was going on? They said, Sylvester Stallone is about fifty yards ahead.

OMG! I couldn't believe it. The man I idolized growing up as a little boy was now fifty yards in front me! Are you serious? I knew this was my moment. I knew this was my chance, but how would I ever meet him when he's surrounded by security guards and thousands of fans? I didn't know the answer, but I did know without a doubt in my mind that I was going to meet him that day. I remembered this amazing story in the Holy Bible:

In Luke 8:43-48, the Holy Bible talks about the woman who had the issue of blood. She wanted her healing. She visualized her healing. She knew that if she could just reach out and touch Jesus she would be healed. However, she had a problem. Jesus was in the middle of thousands of people. That didn't matter to her though. She was determined to make her way through those thousands of people no matter what she had to do. Nothing was going to stop her from getting her healing.

Sure enough, she put The Law Of Attraction to work. She didn't focus on what she didn't want, which was having to get through thousands of people. She only focused on what she did want, which was touching Jesus so she could be healed. She got her healing. What she focused on, which is known as The Law Of Attraction, worked for her, and it will work for you too. The Law Of Attraction works every single time. No exceptions!

My situation was similar. I focused on getting to Sylvester Stallone that day as much as that woman focused on getting to Jesus. I was determined. Nothing was going to stop me. What I focused on, which is known as The Law Of Attraction, worked for me. I got to meet and take my picture with Sylvester Stallone that day. One of my favorite scriptures that I live by every single day is:

Do not conform to the pattern of this world, but be transformed by the renewing of your mind. **Romans 12:2**

This verse tells us not to think the way the rest of the world thinks. The rest of the world would have just given up in these situations. They would have focused on the obstacle, not on the prize. You can have whatever you want in your life if you'll just believe that you can. Focus on what you want, visualize what you want, and believe that it is already yours. See yourself driving your dream car, living in your dream home, and living out all your goals and dreams in life. If you want to get rich and have a lot of money then you need to focus on exactly how much you want. The Law Of Attraction states that whatever you focus on you're going to attract into your life because your thoughts are things.

I was living in Chicago, Illinois back in 2007. While driving to an event my tires ran over some black ice and in a matter of seconds my life would change for the worse. I woke up to the sounds of sirens and the jaws of life cutting my car to pieces to get me and the passenger out of my car. My car was demolished. By the grace of God we lived. It took a while to recover, but today we're both fine.

Over time, I healed physically and started renewing my mind to the word of God. A few months after the accident, I received an offer for a personal trainer position with a company in Florida that would pay me six figures. However, I had a few problems. I didn't have a car, I didn't have any money, and I didn't have good credit. So, how in the world would I be able to get a new car so that I could drive back and forth to my job once I arrived in Florida?

I remembered The Law Of Attraction. I knew that it looked impossible for me to get a new car in the natural, but I also knew that what I focus on I get. So, instead of focusing on not having any money, or good credit, I only focused on getting a new car. At this point in my life I didn't have the prosperous mindset that I have today. So, instead of focusing on a

Lamborghini, I just focused on a lesser priced car. I walked to the Honda dealership in downtown Chicago. I found a brand new, sparkling, red, 2008 Honda Civic sitting on the showroom floor. That's the car I wanted. I accepted it by faith right then and there. A car salesman walked up to me and I told him this was the car I wanted. He told me to follow him back to his desk. He asked me if I had good credit for financing and I told him that I didn't. He then asked me, how do you think you're going to get a brand new car with bad credit? I told him I didn't know how, but I knew that my God would deliver it. He rolled his eyes at me.

He had me fill out a credit application hoping that I might get approved anyway. After he ran my credit he realized I was telling him the truth. He told me there was no way I was going to be able to get that car. I smiled and told him, with God ALL things are possible! I then left the dealership. As I walked away that day, I started visualizing myself sitting in the car, driving the car, and enjoying the car in the Florida sun. This intense focusing is a very real process. When you focus on something with great intensity it makes it feel like you already have the thing that you're focusing on.

I bought a plane ticket from Chicago to Orlando with every last penny that I had. I would arrive in Orlando on Friday and start working at my new job on Monday morning. In my spirit, I just knew, that I knew, that I knew, that somehow, someway, I was going to get that brand new Honda Civic. I just didn't know how. I kept focusing on having the car in my possession. I would leave the rest up to God.

On Friday morning, just hours before flying to Orlando, I received this email from a complete stranger:

Hi Christopher, you don't know me, but I met you a few years ago in Columbus, Ohio at the Arnold Schwarzenegger Bodybuilding Expo. I got a copy of the bodybuilding magazine you were on the cover of that month and you autographed it for me. I only talked to you for a few minutes because other people were waiting in line to meet you. However, you were the nicest bodybuilder I had ever met. I just wanted to say it was a pleasure to meet you. If you ever need anything please feel free to contact me anytime. Sincerely, Bill.

That was the exact email that I received from Bill. The thing that jumped out of his email the most was: If you ever need anything please feel free to contact me anytime. I thought to myself, well, I need a car. So, I decided to email him back and tell him what happened.

I told him I was in a bad car crash. I told him I just got offered a six-figure position as a personal trainer in Florida, but I didn't have a car to get back and forth. I asked him if he was a Christian, and if he was to please pray for me that God would bring me a car. That's all I said to him in my email. He emailed me back within one hour and here's what he said:

Christopher, I'm so sorry to hear about what happened to you. I know you don't know me, but I'm the CEO of a bank. I have perfect credit and plenty of money. You left such an impression on me when I met you that I would be thrilled to buy you a car. Please call me! Sincerely, Bill.

To make a long story short, he told me to go to the Honda dealership once I arrived in Orlando. When I picked out the car that I wanted, call him and put him on the phone with the salesman. He would take care of the rest. I went to the Honda dealership as soon as I arrived in Orlando. I found the same exact, brand new, sparkling, red, 2008 Honda Civic that was sitting on the showroom floor that I saw in the Chicago showroom.

I called Bill, put him on the phone with the car salesman, and two hours later I drove off the car lot with a brand new car without paying a penny for it. It was unbelievable! I drove into an empty parking lot and started to cry. I couldn't believe the way God had come through for me. He used a complete stranger to buy me a brand new car. I think I would have had better odds at winning the lottery than have that happening to me, but it did. God is truly amazing! That story shows you the amazing power of The Law Of Attraction. I focused on getting a brand new car and that's exactly what I attracted.

The Law Of Attraction is a very powerful law that works every single time. You must focus on what you want and believe that you'll receive it. Don't try to figure out "how" you're going to receive it though. That's not your job. Your job is to simply focus on what you want. Leave the "how" to God. That's his part!

Chapter Six:

Confessing Money!

If you want to get rich and have a lot of money, you must start confessing money. Your words have amazing power. Your words can literally change your life. If you'll start confessing money affirmations over your life, more money will come to you. It has to because confession is a law. The Law Of Confession states that the words you speak will manifest in your life because words are seeds.

That's why it's extremely important to only confess things that you want. Never confess things that you don't want. The words you confess on a regular basis will manifest in your life. So, if you want a lot of money, start confessing a lot of money!

Growing up as children we always heard the saying: *sticks and stones will break my bones, but words will never hurt me*. As adults, we know the complete opposite is true. Sticks and stones have never broken any bones, but hurtful words have been known to cause all kinds of illness, sickness, disease, poverty, and unhappiness. Some people have even committed suicide because of hurtful words that someone spoke to them. Words have amazing power!

Children who have parents that speak negatively to them all the time grow up with inferiority complexes. If you're a parent make sure that you only confess positive words over your children. Encourage them with your words. Remind them with your words that they're blessed and they can achieve anything they set their mind to. Build them up with your words.

Did you know that you can make yourself rich or poor by the words that you confess every day? It's true! I can tell whether someone is rich or poor by simply talking to them for just sixty seconds. The words that they speak will tell me. Do you ever pay attention to how poor people speak? If you do, you'll notice that poor people always say things like:

-I can't afford that.

-Money is the root of all evil.

-Money doesn't grow on trees.

-I'd rather be happy than be rich.

Every time a person confesses something negative about money, they're only cursing themselves financially. If you want to stay poor forever keep on confessing words of poverty over your life. That's a guarantee that you will stay poor.

Instead of confessing how poor you are all the time, start confessing how rich you are. Jesus came to give us life and give it to us in abundance. Abundance isn't living a life of barely paying your bills! Abundance is living a life of not having any bills. Living a life of abundance means that all your needs are met, you're completely out of debt, and you have a whole lot more to put in store for others. You deserve to live a life of abundance. Abundance begins with your mouth!

Start confessing what the Holy Bible says about money instead of what the world says. Let me tell you what the Holy Bible says about money so you can start confessing it yourself:

May the Lord, the God of my ancestors, increase me a thousand times and bless me as he has promised! **Deuteronomy 1:11**

I will remember the Lord my God, for it is he who gives me the ability to produce wealth, and so confirms his covenant, which he swore to my ancestors, as it is today.
Deuteronomy 8:18

The Lord will grant me abundant prosperity! **Deuteronomy 28:11**

With me are riches and honor, enduring wealth and prosperity.
Proverbs 8:18

The blessing of the Lord brings me wealth without painful toil for it.
Proverbs 10:22

God gives me hidden treasures, riches stored in secret places, so that I know that he is the Lord. **Isaiah 45:3**

God gives me wealth and possessions and the ability to enjoy them. This is a gift of God. **Ecclesiastes 5:19**

Whatever you want to achieve in life is what you need to start confessing. If you want to get a new car, then start confessing that. If you want to move into a new home, then start confessing that. For the purpose of this book, let's stay focused on money. If you want a lot of money, then start confessing that. Here are some of my personal money confessions that I speak over and over throughout the day. You're welcome to start confessing these for yourself or you can create your own.

-I am infinite money!

-Show me the money!

-Money comes to me easily and effortlessly!

-I love money and money loves me, money comes to me easily!

Another powerful money strategy is the "I Am" principle. "I Am" are two of the most powerful words in the English language. Whatever you confess after these two words will manifest in your life. Most people only confess negative words when they unconsciously use this principle and they wonder why their lives are in disarray. By consciously changing the words you confess after the phrase "I Am", you can significantly change your life forever.

Here are some of my personal "I Am" phrases that I confess every day:

-I am rich!

-I am wealthy!

-I am successful!

-I am truly blessed!

-I am a multi-millionaire!

The words that come out of your mouth every day will manifest in your life because your words are seeds. This is a spiritual law that works for every person in the world. You must remember this! You can change any circumstance you're going through in life simply by changing your words and believing what you confess.

You can get yourself out of debt by using The Law Of Confession. Simply take your debt papers in your hands, whatever they may be (loan for a car, loan for a mortgage, student loans, credit card debt, etc.) and confess over them. COMMAND them to be eliminated! COMMAND them to be paid off in full! COMMAND them to disappear and never come back! This is how The Law Of Confession works! You must believe in this law and what you confess in order for it to work.

Jesus even told his disciples about the powerful Law Of Confession in the Holy Bible in the book of Mark:

*The next day as they were leaving Bethany, Jesus was hungry. Seeing in the distance a fig tree in leaf, he went to find out if it had any fruit. When he reached it, he found nothing but leaves, because it was not the season for figs. Then he **SAID** to the tree, may no one ever eat fruit from you again. His disciples heard him say it.*
Mark 11:12-14

If Jesus himself tells you that your words can change your life then you better believe it to be true.

*Truly I tell you, if anyone **SAYS** to this mountain, Go, throw yourself into the sea, and does not doubt in their heart, but believes what they **SAY** will happen, it will be done for them.*
Mark 11:23

Chapter Seven:

Associate With Money!

When I say "Associate With Money" I'm strongly encouraging you to live by The Law Of Association. This law states that who you associate with is who you'll become. If you associate with people who drink alcohol every day then you're going to drink alcohol every day too. If you associate with people who are poor financially then you're going to be poor financially too. However, if you associate with millionaires and billionaires, guess what? You're going to become one!

This is how The Law Of Association works. The people you associate with will rub off on you. They will leave an impression on you and you'll want to impress them back so that you can be accepted by them. You'll follow them and do what they do so you can fit in with them, whether you like how they live their lives or not. This is peer pressure and it's more prevalent with adults than it is with children. This is why freshman in high school begin smoking cigarettes. They want to impress and fit in with the upper classmen. However, if you would have asked them when they were in the eighth grade if they would like a cigarette they would have told you absolutely not. Things change when it comes to associations.

This is why it is extremely important to associate with money. When you associate with people who have a lot of money you'll learn why. You'll find that they speak and think differently about money than poor people do. This is why they're rich. As you listen to them speak you'll notice how they speak about money. Poor people and rich people don't mix well around each other because they don't have anything to talk about. They have nothing in common. Remember the famous quotation that says:

Birds of a feather flock together?

Well, now you know what this means. You'll never see chickens associating with eagles. They're completely different. They have nothing in common. Chickens are like poor people. They're very depressing to be around. They don't think big or even dream. Every word that comes out of their mouths are negative. All they do is peck on the ground all day.

Eagles however, are like rich people. They're very rare. They don't ever peck on the ground. They don't even fly. They soar! They can climb to higher altitudes than airplanes. They like to be above their prey. They like to be on top of the world. They have laser beam focus and can see their target from a mile away. They set their eyes on what they want and go toward it with pin point accuracy.

Rich people are highly focused. They set goals and do whatever it takes to achieve them. You'll never see them slacking off or hear them complain. They let their actions do the talking for them. While poor people (chickens) are easily distracted, rich people know exactly what they want. These are qualities of the rich. By associating with rich people their habits and mindsets will help you grow and develop into a leader. You can have a sixty second conversation with someone and know if they're rich or poor. The words that come out of people's mouths will tell you everything about them.

If you want to become rich you must associate with rich people. That's all there is to it. Associating with people who have a lot more money than you do will increase your thinking and catapult your income. We become like the people we associate with. That's why winners are attracted to winners. The only reason why a few people become millionaires and billions is because they speak and think differently about money. That's why you need to listen closely to the people you associate with. The words they speak will tell you who they are. Let me give you a few examples so you know who to associate with and who not to associate with.

Poor people say, I hate my job!

Rich people say, I love my business!

Poor people say, I just got a forty cent raise at my job.

Rich people say, I just increased my net worth by twenty million dollars.

Poor people say, I really need a vacation.

Rich people say, I should end this vacation and get back to work.

Poor people say, I can't wait to get paid on Friday so I can buy a new big screen television.

Rich people say, I can't wait to sell my company so I can use the cash to invest in a bigger one.

Poor people say, I'm going to drive the family to the lake this weekend.

Rich people say, I'm going to fly the family to Tahiti this weekend.

Obviously, you can clearly see the difference. These are the types of words you need to listen for. The words that come out of a person's mouth will tell you if a person is rich or poor. If you want to get rich you must associate with rich people as much as possible. Poor people want to meet a millionaire so they can tell their friends they met a millionaire. However, millionaires want to associate with billionaires so they can learn how they think. Poor people are in the stands watching the game. Rich people are on the field playing the game. Which one are you?

You need to write down the top five people in your life that you associate with the most. Take their incomes, add them together, then divide the number by five. The number that appears will be so close to the income you make it will scare you.

That's why you must associate with rich people. If you spend all your time with four different millionaires, guess what? Pretty soon you'll be the fifth millionaire. This is how The Law Of Association works.

Everyone knows this is true. Big, strong bodybuilders associate with other big, strong bodybuilders. Religious people associate with other religious people. And of course, rich people associate with other rich people. Again, birds of a feather flock together. So, start associating with rich people and you'll become rich. Rich people are always looking for individuals who are optimistic, goal-oriented, enthusiastic, and who have a positive mental outlook on life. However, on the flip side, rich people do everything in their power to avoid people who are toxic and negative.

Chapter Eight:

Visualize Money!

Visualize money means that you form images or pictures in your mind about money. You must believe that you are worthy of having a lot of money. Once you believe that you'll have a lot money is when you'll actually see the money come into your life. You must see yourself having a lot of money in your mind before you will ever see it show up in the natural, physical world.

Poor people always say that when they see it then they'll believe it, but is it any wonder why they never see money show up? Because they didn't believe the money would show up. They were waiting to see it until they believed it, but that's why they're poor. They have it backwards.

However, rich people understand this. They believed in their minds when they were dead broke that they would be rich someday. It was this belief that allowed the money to show up physically. You must believe the money will show up before you'll ever see it show up. You must always remember this! In order to increase your confidence and belief that a lot of money will come into your life you need to change your mind set about money. A great way of doing this is by reading books that talk about money. Until I started associating with rich people I had never read a book in my life, let alone a book about money. However, from the moment I read my first book about money I was hooked. I couldn't get enough. Now, I've read hundreds of books about money. Reading this many books has changed my mind set about money.

Here's a list of some of my personal favorite books that I've read about money that will have a big impact on how you think about money:

The Holy Bible.

Prosperity: Charles Fillmore.

Money Cometh: Leroy Thompson.

Rich Dad Poor Dad: Robert Kiyosaki.

Think And Grow Rich: Napoleon Hill.

First Steps To Wealth: Dani Johnson.

The Secret Of The Ages: Robert Collier.

The Blessing Of The Lord: Kenneth Copeland.

The Magic Of Thinking Big: David Schwartz.

The Power Of Positive Thinking: Norman Vincent Peale.

Once you develop the right mind set about money you will then be able to attract money into your life in huge amounts. I also encourage you to make a vision board. This is a big white board that you can get at the grocery store. The idea is to build your dream lifestyle on this board by taping up pictures of everything you desire in your life. On my vision board I have pictures of millions of dollars in hundred dollar bills, luxury sports cars, luxury mansions, tropical vacation spots, and the charities that I contribute to. I look at my vision board every day and visualize myself living this lifestyle in my mind.

Another thing you can do is to write out money affirmations every day. By confessing, visualizing, and writing out your money affirmations, you give your mind several different ways to absorb the lifestyle that you want.

The money confessions that I shared with you in chapter six are the same confessions that I write down on paper every day in the form of my money affirmations. Here are my money confessions again:

-I am infinite money!

-Show me the money!

-Money comes to me easily and effortlessly!

-I love money and money loves me, money comes to me easily!

So, not only do I confess these every day with my mouth, but I also write them down on paper as well. I'll write these down for a minimum of ten times each, sometimes many more. There's nothing fancy about it. I'm just programming my mind for money. Here's what it looks like:

1. I am infinite money!

2. I am infinite money!

3. I am infinite money!

4. I am infinite money!

5. I am infinite money!

6. I am infinite money!

7. I am infinite money!

8. I am infinite money!

9. I am infinite money!

10. I am infinite money!

Don't think this visualization exercise is stupid or pointless. That's what poor people think, which keeps them from doing it, and they continue to stay poor. However, rich people love doing things like this on a regular basis. They'll tell you this is what has reprogrammed their mind set from one of poverty to wealth.

Here's a visualization method you can use to focus on what you want in life. Lay down on your back in a quiet place with no distractions. Imagine yourself laying on the shore of the ocean. Your feet are closest to the water. Inhale deep breaths. As you breathe in, imagine the waves are coming in toward you. As you breathe out, imagine the waves going back out to sea. With every breath that you take calm those waves down until the water is completely still.

Now your breathing should be very relaxed. This is a deep meditative state that you're in. Now, begin to visualize the life you want. See yourself driving your dream car, living in your dream home, having the perfect physical body, traveling the world to all your favorite places, and giving millions of dollars away to the needy. Whatever it is that you desire

71

in life, visualize it and make it real right now! The more you visualize the life you want, the faster it will manifest in your physical world. Visualization is a powerful process that can truly change your life. Just be consistent with it and do it on a regular basis. What you can see in your mind, you can have in your life.

Chapter Nine:

Give Away Money!

I know this might sound contrary to getting rich, but giving away money will actually bring in more money. The Law Of Sowing And Reaping states that what you sow you reap. This is also known as The Law Of Giving And Receiving. What you give you will receive. The Holy Bible says:

Give, and it will be given to you. A good measure, pressed down, shaken together and running over, will be poured into your lap. For with the measure you use, it will be measured to you. **Luke 6:38**

This is another reason why you must get rich and have a lot of money. People who don't have money can't give any away. This reason alone should motivate you to become rich.

I made it my mission in life when I was only seven years old to become extremely wealthy, simply because, I knew that the more money I brought in meant the more money I could give away. I also knew that the best thing I could do for the poor was not to be one of them. My entire life, I've always believed that poor people are selfish people because they only think about themselves. If they thought about other people that would motivate them to become rich. Any excess money that they don't need they can simply give away to others who do need it.

Research has proven that people who give away money to others and to different charities experience more happiness than those who don't give. Not only does giving away money make a person happier, but it makes them wealthier too. Whatever you give away has to come back to you multiplied even more. That's what The Law Of Giving And Receiving states. Every philanthropist says the reason why they give away their money is because it makes them happier and wealthier. Bill Ackman is a hedge fund billionaire. Here's what he said about giving away his money:

While my motivations for giving are not driven by a profit motive, I am quite sure that I have earned financial returns from giving away money. Not directly by any means, but as a result of the people I've met, the ideas I've been exposed to, and from the experiences I've had as a result of giving away money. I met a number of my closest friends, partners and advisers from my charitable giving. The more money I give away the richer my life becomes.

Every successful mentor that I've ever had told me once I become successful financially, I must be generous with my money by giving it away to people who are less fortunate. The greatest book ever written about money, the Holy Bible, also says that people who are generous with their money will always have an abundance of it.

One person gives freely, yet gains even more, another withholds unduly, but comes to poverty. **Proverbs 11:24**

A generous person will prosper; whoever refreshes others will be refreshed. **Proverbs 11:25**

Whoever is kind to the poor lends to the Lord, and he will reward them for what they have done. **Proverbs 19:17**

The generous will themselves be blessed, for they share their food with the poor. **Proverbs 22:9**

My final words are **give away money**! If you're poor right now that's the perfect reason to start giving. Almost every person who is wealthy today was poor at one time in their life. However, instead of making excuses as to why they couldn't afford to give, they made up their minds that they couldn't afford not to give. They knew if they didn't give when they were poor, they would never get rich.

Remember this: Whoever sows sparingly will also reap sparingly, and whoever sows generously will also reap generously. Each of you should give what you have decided in your heart to give, not reluctantly or under compulsion, for God loves a cheerful giver. And God is able to bless you abundantly, so that in all things at all times, having all that you need, you will abound in every good work.
2 Corinthians 9:6-8

Now that you've read this book would you mind doing me a big favor please? Would you be kind enough to write me a five star customer review for this book on Amazon? By giving this book a good review it will help me as an author and help this book move up the rankings on Amazon. Your words have power. If you wouldn't mind supporting this book I would be extremely grateful. I would love to hear your feedback. You're welcome to contact me at my website anytime. If you would appreciate me sending you valuable, life changing tips for free through email, please feel free to subscribe with your name and email address on my website below. I wish you all the best! God bless you!

Christopher Mitchell

www.ChangeYourLifeOvernight.com

If you enjoyed reading this book, here's more books by the author:

1. How To Lose Weight With Intermittent Fasting!

2. Sell Your First Book!

3. The #1 How To Get Rich Book For Christian Men & Women!

4. My Inspiring True Life Story!

5. How To Get Rich From Home On A Part Time Basis With Only $20!

6. Why You're Fat & Sick And How To Fix It!

7. Success! The Secret To Becoming Happy, Healthy, And Wealthy!

8. How To Make Money As An Author Selling Your Books On Amazon!

9. Faith Produces Miracles!

All books can be purchased from:
www.ChangeYourLifeOvernight.com